the gay & lesbian guide to (and from) betrayal

**The Journal
for Gays & Lesbians
Suffering the Pains of a Love Triangle**

ELISSA GOUGH

© 1998 Face Reality, Inc.™

The Gay & Lesbian Guide to (and from) Betrayal
Elissa Gough

Face Reality, Inc.™
P.O. Box 8593
Cincinnati, Ohio 45208-0593

1-800-5AFFAIR (phone)
1-513-871-4999 (fax)

info@facereality.com (email)
www.facereality.com (www)

LCCN 98-092438
ISBN 1-891863-06-1

Attention Organizations, licensed, practicing care-givers and schools:
Quantity discounts are available on bulk purchases of this book for educational purposes or fund raising. Special books or book excerpts can also be created to fit specific needs. For information, contact Face Reality, Inc., P.O. Box 8593, Cincinnati, Ohio 45208-0593 or call 1-800-5AFFAIR / fax (513) 871-4999.

ACKNOWLEDGMENT

This journal would not have been possible without the help and support of my gay and lesbian friends and acquaintances.

I deeply appreciate their openness and willingness to help make certain this journal is relevant to their lives.

CONGRATULATIONS!

Whether you've chosen this journal for yourself or someone else, you have taken an essential step to know more about the subject of betrayal in long-term committed relationships.

introduction

Betrayal is highly exploited, controversial and certainly discussed a great deal. You wonder, *Who is doing it? Should I do it? Why aren't I doing it?* **In the process, you can try to deny your thoughts and feelings, yet they don't actually leave you.**

Cheating is betrayal, and it's as old as civilization. Each of you is tempted and tested at some point in your life. It doesn't really matter who you are or what kind of person you consider yourself to be, this action is a cry for help from a hurting person. Unfaithfulness is a symptom that something in your life is not right and needs attention and resolution. One person might choose to drink, another to overeat, but the common threads are the unresolved, hurting issues that crop up, again and again.

Many in those fairy tales lived happily ever after; **why not you?**

Are you just flirting with the idea of straying? Maybe you or someone you know is in the throes of an affair or at the end of a long road of unfaithfulness, wanting to break the cycle. Regardless of where you find yourself, this journal will help you see the realities...not the fantasies that are typically played out as affairs escalate.

Affairs can be prevented, when you start with the consequences first and work your way back to that fateful decision to begin an affair. By following this approach, you will be spared the heart-wrenching consequences that accompany the thrills and temporary excitement that affairs create.

Today, your challenge is to make a choice regarding unfaithfulness. You can keep chasing your fantasies that are based on deceit, lies and destruction, or you can become more informed, knowledgeable and resistant to this temptation as you come to grips with your situation.

Isn't it Time You Face Reality?

▼contents

journalizing

"*The discipline of the written word punishes both stupidity and dishonesty.*"

John Steinbeck

It's Probably Harder When You Are Gay or Lesbian.

It's a tangled web you might find yourself caught in today. Trying to live your life as a homosexual can, in itself, be a tremendous challenge. Include the torrent of feelings and emotions that accompany betrayal and your life will soon become overwhelming. Whether you are **the one cheating**, **the one being betrayed**, or if you find yourself on the third side of the triangle as the **"new lover"** — positive help and support is crucial, in order to get your life back under control.

Depending on your personal history and the part of the country and community you live in, your sexual preference can fall somewhere between *a source of pride* and *a dark secret.* Unfortunately, if you're in the vast majority, it probably falls closer to the "dark secret" end of the spectrum. Gays and lesbians are often discriminated against, either overtly or subtly, by business communities, law enforcement, government housing authorities, religious institutions, educators and a raft of others.

There continues to be senseless hurt, cruelty and prejudice. Sometimes you're responsible, but you usually have little or no control over situations. Too often, emotional and physical abuse enter your life. Unless you're fortunate enough to connect with a gay or lesbian counselor, a straight therapist who understands your circumstances or close friends who are willing to help, you may find that your only option is to seek advice from others who are struggling with the same emotional turmoil in their long-term relationships.

When your stressful life is further complicated by unfaithfulness, positive emotional support can be very difficult to find and ultimately accept. Fortunately, more resources are becoming available today, especially in large urban areas, where local homosexual-rights organizations are plentiful.

▼ Your triangle can be one of the most fragile.

Legal vows and community standards do not often support your relationship. For many, just the process of *coming out* and letting those close to you know your sexual orientation can be fearful, as well as emotionally painful to face. You can quickly lose control of your life when your situation is further challenged by an affair.

Gay and lesbian relationships experience many of the same problems found in heterosexual triangles. Added stress is created when a player in your triangle feels the need to maintain secrecy about his or her sexuality. **One partner is breaking a solemn vow of loyalty, another is betrayed by the person he or she loves and trusts most, and the third person is thought of as the most coveted, intrusive member in the relationship.**

Regardless of your role in your particular triangle, an affair will cost you dearly in time, emotional stress, self-esteem and cold cash. Usually, outside of counseling, your circle of friends, or various limited support groups, there aren't many places to go when you reach the limits of fear, pain and disgust that betrayal initiates.

Are you worried that your long-term partner will step out with a stranger?

How much time are you spending alone, left behind, hoping the phone will ring, waiting for your lover to sneak away or getting ready to rendezvous?

What lies are you telling and being told?

Do you need to hide your sexuality for your lover's sake?

How many broken promises do you continue to accept?

Do you feel you're wasting the best years of your life?

Are you at risk for sexually transmitted diseases (STD)?

The answers to questions like these and many others may be careening around inside your head as you battle the world of betrayal.

Use this journal to help you focus on these issues and make positive decisions regarding your particular situation.

IT'S TIME TO OVERCOME THE ODDS –
regardless of what role you claim in your triangle.

▼ Betrayal and Unfaithfulness in the Gay Community.

Unfaithfulness crosses all walks of life. It's blind to race, age, socio-economic status and sexual orientation. For the gay population, however, cheating often includes characteristics unique to same-sex relationships. The following generalizations are not true of every triangle of betrayal, but they're common to many.

▼ betrayal *in* general...

- ▼ ...is not the thrilling, carefree ride the entertainment industry portrays.
- ▼ ...is often difficult to keep secret.
- ▼ ...results in pain and suffering for the immediate spectators (betrayed) as well as the participants.
- ▼ ...creates a ripple effect that's felt by extended family members, friends, neighbors and coworkers.
- ▼ ...can quickly lead to emotional and financial devastation.
- ▼ ...causes serious harm to one's integrity and self-esteem.
- ▼ ...can cost someone their job and has the ability to damage their career and professional reputation.
- ▼ ...requires a great deal of deception and lying.
- ▼ ...introduces the risk of STD to previously monogamous relationships.
- ▼ ...will bring out the worst in people — weaknesses in coping skills, emotional instability, paranoia, and tendencies for violent behavior.
- ▼ ...doesn't resolve those old hurts that are at the heart of the matter.
- ▼ ...creates additional problems and new conflicts in the triangle.
- ▼ ...is driven by the need to find an ideal partner/mate.

▼ betrayal among gays & lesbians

- ▼ ...can be cruelly stereotyped by the media and society in general, as behavior expected of most homosexuals.
- ▼ ...is more of a challenge to keep secret, because of the greater tendency to gossip, in your closely-knit communities.
- ▼ ...is often met with resistance and a lack of support from family and friends.
- ▼ ...can escalate to violent outbursts and physical abuse.
- ▼ ...is often treated with ridicule by law-enforcement personnel called in to protect one party from the other.
- ▼ ...can be more complicated in bisexual triangles.
- ▼ ...is likely to be motivated by the sexual desire for multiple partners.
- ▼ ...is openly discussed with friends and acquaintances rather than kept hidden.

▼ gays (Men) & lesbians (Women)
See Things Differently.

WOMEN USUALLY...

▼ ...seek therapy more readily.

▼ ...need to feel cared for prior to having sex.

▼ ...want their partner to give of her time, and be a good listener.

▼ ...dissect relationships more methodically.

▼ ...are capable of becoming expert liars.

▼ ...ultimately, feel the financial impact and emotional pain as a direct consequence of breaking up.

▼ ...think it over more extensively before having an affair.

▼ ...tolerate a dysfunctional relationship longer.

▼ ...suspect an affair, based on the least bit of evidence, and then continue to search for more clues.

WOMEN IN AFFAIRS USUALLY...

▼ ...enter an affair in spite of their concern for the consequences.

▼ ...lead with their heart and strive for a commitment from their lovers.

▼ ...feel a need to share their affairs with trusted friends, at length over and over.

▼ ...seek validation of their affairs from others.

▼ ...do not consider sex with a man (bi-sexuality) to be cheating.

▼ ...allow their affairs to consume their entire lives.

WOMEN WHOSE PARTNERS ARE IN AFFAIRS USUALLY...

▼ ...use the affair as an excuse for irrational behavior and uncontrollable emotional outbursts.

▼ ...expect their long-term partner to share details of her new relationship.

▼ ...can retaliate by having affairs themselves.

▼ ...spend a great deal of time obsessing over their partner's affair.

▼ ...are threatened by the new lover and often feel the need to put her down.

▼ ...will seldom forgive and forget, often bringing it up years after an affair has ended.

▼ ...consider the affair to be an unforgivable violation of their relationship vows, when it's their partners who are unfaithful.

▼ ...will not respect their partner's privacy when looking for clues. (open private mail, search clothing and cars, listen to phone conversations)

▼ ...are more apt to hire a detective when cheating is suspected.

▼ ...confront their cheating partner, and will often confront the new lover.

▼ ...feel their partner's sharing of personal information is as much a violation of their relationship as the sexual acts of betrayal.

▼ ...see financial devastation for their partner's betrayal as justifiable.

▼ ...degrade their partner to any children involved, because of their own hurt.

▼ ...want their children to "tell all" they know of their mate's illicit escapades.

▼ ...expect their partners to leave home immediately when the affair is exposed, but demand the participant continue meeting all financial responsibilities.

▼ ...blame the new lover for the affair, rather than their long-term partner.

▼ ...will rarely recognize their own degree of responsibility for their partner's cheating: "Why me?" "How could she do this to me?"

▼ ...assume the role of victim, remaining trapped in that state indefinitely.

▼ ...feel the need to form an army of family and/or friends for support.

▼ ...hope their partner's affairs have ended or deny it's happening.

▼ ...often reject apologies from their partners as a final solution to the situation.

▼ ...find it easier to love again than to trust again.

▼ ...turn the other cheek for a time.

MEN USUALLY...

▼ ...have a low threshold for an unhappy relationship and will seek someone else as a means of coping.

▼ ...are reluctant to seek therapy, and will agree only as a last resort.

▼ ...want *sex* first, and then fall in love.

▼ ...are expert liars in affairs.

MEN IN AFFAIRS USUALLY...

▼ ...enter their triangle without much thought to the final consequences.

▼ ...are quick to rationalize their betrayal: *"I can handle it." "It just happened."*

▼ ...look for different qualities in an illicit lover than the qualities they desire for a long-term partner.

▼ ...begin their affairs out of passion and conquest, wanting some variety.

▼ ...enjoy the chase and challenge, like a game.

▼ ...try to conduct their relationships in a detached, cavalier manner.

▼ ...consider any affair to be a forgivable violation of the relationship vows.

▼ ...don't keep their affairs a secret (unlike heterosexual men).

▼ ...are not interested in understanding the *whys* of an affair — why it started, why it continues, why it's hurtful, and why it should end.

▼ ...deny it, even when caught.

▼ ...get sloppy over time, leaving obvious clues that cause them to be exposed.

▼ ...will say their relationship is over, when they have no intention of ending it.

▼ ...consider apologies to their partners sufficient action for forgiveness.

▼ ...underestimate how their partners will react.

▼ ...don't expect break-ups as a consequence.

▼ ...are shocked when their partners walk out or when they are expected to leave home immediately.

▼ ...rarely admit their affair caused the end of their long-term relationship.

▼ ...don't consider sex with a woman to be cheating on their partners.

▼ ...are more apt to leave their spouses or partners when they have someone waiting for them.

MEN WHOSE PARTNERS ARE IN AFFAIRS USUALLY...

▼ ...consider cheating by the partner far more serious than their own unfaithfulness.

▼ ...suspect a partner's cheating, long before it's exposed.

▼ ...consider sex by their partners forgivable and often turn the other cheek when deeply in love.

▼ ...want psychological pain, suffering, and material penalties for their mate, as paybacks for their unfaithfulness.

▼ ...are unable to get past the affair and rehash it over and over.

▼ ...rationalize their partner's affair as justification for their own affair.

▼ ...leave the relationship, in order to regain their self-respect and block their resolved pain.

▼ ...want answers to their questions, including specific details regarding their partner's affair and his new lover.

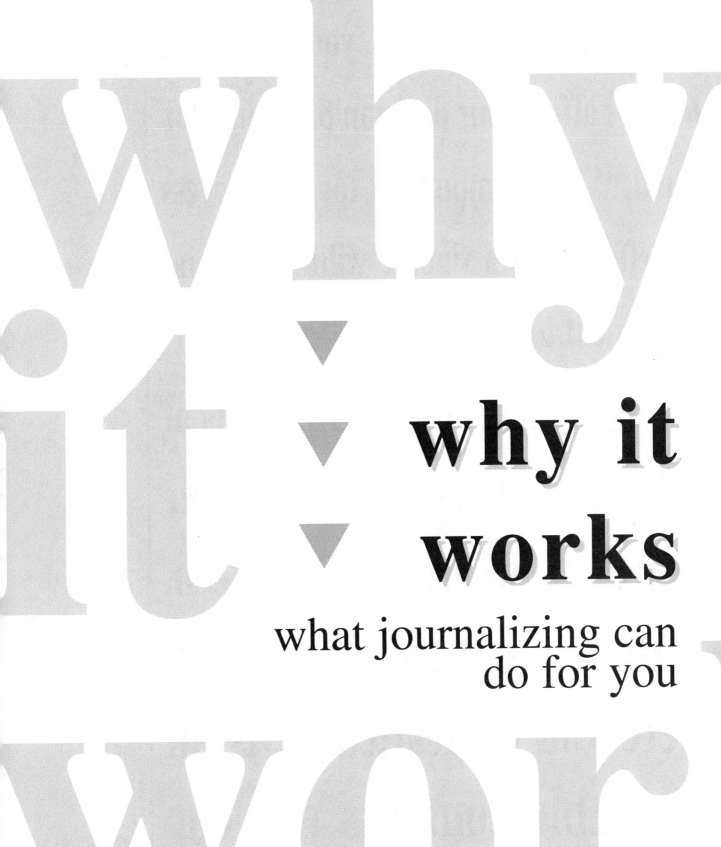

why it
works

what journalizing can do for you

The current status of your situation shouldn't affect your decision to begin your journal. What is important for the process to be effective is a sincere willingness and commitment to write.

You will benefit from journalizing at any time, as writing presents a clearer picture of where you've been, where you currently are, and where you're headed. It is an invaluable compass on your journey of self-discovery.

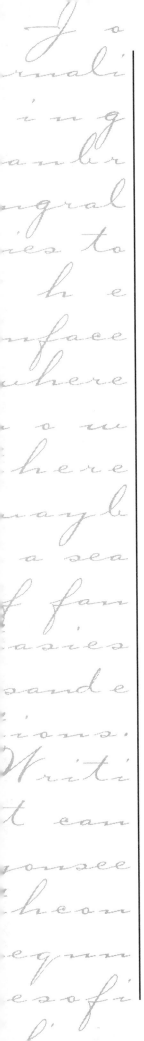

What the Purpose Is and Why It Works!

It was only after years of my infidelity that I made a decision to keep daily entries of my experiences. My reason for getting started was probably more to validate my behavior and feelings rather than to understand or possibly change ways of handling situations. Those entries gave me a place to vent my frustrations and anger as well as immortalize the joyful and memorable events.

Over time, I began to recognize patterns in my behavior and saw how I could change. I started to face my fears more confidently, choosing my direction with wisdom instead of reacting to circumstances by impulse. Writing became a way of life for me.

It is private and anonymous.

▼ It can be written in secrecy. No one else reads it unless given permission.
▼ Confidentiality is respected. Hiding your journal should not be difficult. (After all, you've kept your affair a secret, haven't you?)
▼ There's no need to fear or be concerned with how you look to others or how they might be affected as you write.

It is self-administered.

▼ You can begin using it immediately, without the involvement of anyone.
▼ It gives you the advantage of engaging in daily conversations with yourself as you express and reveal your innermost thoughts & feelings openly & honestly.
▼ Writing spares repeated dialogues with friends each day regarding your affair or the unfaithfulness of your mate or partner.

It keeps personal confrontations to a minimum.

▼ It's a great way to unload excess baggage without face-to-face contact.
▼ You'll have a chance to evaluate your motives and strategies before you act.
▼ Do you tend to be impulsive? This will help you re-think your responses.
▼ It provides an appreciation of the viewpoints of others involved in the affair.
▼ Pent-up anger can lead to violent outbursts; your journal gives you a place to vent and work through your fury.

It is a practical extension or alternative to therapy.

▼ If you are not in counseling/therapy, here's a positive outlet for issues you might typically share.

▼ It works in conjunction with or as an alternative to counseling/therapy.

▼ Your entries become valuable references for your feelings. Together, you can discuss them in therapy, if you choose.

▼ Put yourself first. Figure out what *you* need, without being overly concerned with what others expect of you.

▼ If you participate in a seminar or workshop, your journal will prepare you to get the most out of the experience. As you become more in touch with your feelings through writing, you'll have confidence discussing your situation with others.

It brings discipline at a time when you need it the most and creates a blueprint of understanding.

▼ Write each day if you want to capture a realistic picture of your particular situation. The more detailed your entries, the more information you'll have available to evaluate.

▼ Routine is important. Try to select the same time and place daily where you will be uninterrupted. Creating order out of chaos takes responsibility. This is a time in your life when structure is greatly needed.

It will help you foresee the consequences of your actions.

▼ Can you usually predict the outcome when a friend tells you a story? Now you're writing your own story, as you gain the ability to see where you're headed and, if possible, avoid disaster. You'll better understand your situation and the behavior provoking your responses.

▼ You will be able to track your part in the progression of the affair by writing each day. *Why did this affair happen? What are you getting from it now? Where is it headed? Where will it leave you in the long run?*

▼ Reflect over your entries often, in order to avoid repeating mistakes. Feelings, attitudes and ways of responding change over time as you heal and recover.

doing it.

Getting Down

To The Business

of Journalizing

To thine ownself be true,

And it must follow, as the night the day,

Thou canst not then be false to any man.

Shakespeare, *Hamlet*

Here's How it Works.

1. Complete the exercises.

The first one, "*A Blinding Flash of the Obvious*," will help you record essential aspects of the betrayal. The questions are divided into three categories; just answer the **two** that apply to you:

▼ **Most Gays and Lesbians** *and*

▼ **Gays and Lesbians in Long-Term Relationships** *or*

▼ **The Third "Player" in the Triangle**

Your responsibility is to fill-in the answers — the only ground rule is *no more lies*. When you've completed the questions, you'll have insight into the hows and whys of the affair, where your own relationship is headed, and the consequences you can expect.

The second exercise, "*Creative Writing 101*," gives you an opportunity to vent your frustrations and concerns. This exercise has three categories. Select the one that best describes your situation:

▼ **The One Being Betrayed**

▼ **The One Doing the Cheating**

▼ **The New Lover**

Now complete the exercises in the category that applies to you. Compose some letters you won't actually send and write some classified ads you won't really place. The experience is positively liberating!

2. Write daily entries.

There's a glossary (page 60) to help you understand the kinds of issues your writing should examine. Use it for a quick reference initially, to keep your ideas on track.

3. Read what you wrote.

Every week or two, refer back to the beginning of your daily entries and review them. Then read your answers in *A Blinding Flash of the Obvious* and *Creative Writing 101*. Do you feel differently about your responses? They have a way of changing over time.

a blinding flash
Obvious *of the*

A Private Act of Courage

You openly reveal aspects of yourself to others in your work relationships, as well as with your family and friends daily, but how often do you dare to take a look inward?

Here's your chance. There are no right or wrong answers. There's just *your* story. The more candid you are as you complete the questions, the more revealing and helpful they will become.

If you aren't sure of every question, haven't the time, or simply don't want to now, go back to them later. You may choose to work through all the exercises before beginning your daily entries, or you can begin them immediately.

Select whatever pace is most comfortable for you, but go through them.

(Complete the sections that apply to you. For the sake of simplicity, the word "homosexual" is used to refer to gays and lesbians. You may want to read the whole section a few times before you write down your answers.)

▼ Most Gays and Lesbians

History

1. At what age did you realize your homosexuality ? _____

2. Have you ever been sexually or physically abused? _____

If yes, how and at what age? _____

_____

_____

By a member of the same or opposite sex? _____

How did you overcome the experience? _____

_____

_____

3. Have you ever been raped? _____

By a member of the same or opposite sex? _____

How did you work through the experience? _____

_____

_____

4. Do you think your sexual orientation might ever change? Why? _____

_____

Have you tried to change it? What happened? _____

_____

_____

5. How old were you when you had your first sexual experience? _____

(where one or both of you reached orgasm)? _____

How many partners have you had, not including your current partner(s)? ____

6. Have you ever been married or had a heterosexual partner in a committed relationship? If yes, how many times and how did that make you feel? ____

Were you pursuing a same-sex lover at the time? _____

7. Were either of your parents unfaithful to each other, or another partner? How did you know? _____

Your Life

8. Does your immediate family know your sexual orientation? If yes, how did they find out? What was their reaction? _____

_____

Are they supportive of you? _____ **If no, do you plan to share your secret? When?** _____

9. Do you conceal your homosexuality from your daily acquaintances? If yes, who? Your friends, co-workers, employer, landlord, neighbors, teachers, fellow students, etc.? Why? _____

_____

10. Have you ever been discriminated against because of your sexual preference? If yes, how? _____

11. Do you regularly use drugs or alcohol when you are having sex? If yes, why?

_____

_____

12. Does the risk of AIDS affect your sexual activities? If yes, why? _____

_____

Beliefs

13. How do you define betrayal (unfaithfulness)? _____

14. Do society's biases regarding homosexuality affect the intensity of your same-sex relationships? If yes, how? _____

_____

15. Do you think cheating is *more* or *less* a serious betrayal when it occurs in a same-sex relationship? _____

_____

16. Are you typically the more dominant or submissive partner in your relationships? Are you comfortable with that role? _____

_____

17. Does your dominant or submissive role in the partnership play a factor in your attitudes regarding monogamy? _____

_____

18. Do you have specific religious or spiritual beliefs? Do you practice them?

_____

19. Would you choose a long-term monogamous relationship with someone you love if you could? If yes, why? _____

_____

▼Gays and Lesbians in Long-Term Relationships

Your Affair

1. How did you meet your lover/partner? When did you meet? Is this your first homosexual relationship? _____

2. How did you discover the sexual preference of this long-term partner when you first met? Is he/she exclusively homosexual? Are you? _____

3. What did you ask before you shared sex? What questions would you ask today, if you had the opportunity to go back in time to when you first met? _____

4. Are you practicing safe sex? _____
5. How long did you know each other before you had sex for the first time? _____

Your Relationship

6. Is this your first *long-term* relationship? _____
If no, how many have there been? _____
7. How long have you been in this relationship? _____
8. Why did you choose this partner? _____

9. What qualities do you admire in this person? Were these the qualities that attracted you to this person in the beginning? How have they changed? _____

10. Why do you feel this individual chose you? _____

11. What qualities do you feel he/she admires in you? Do you think these are the same qualities that attracted your partner to you when you first met?

12. What "baggage" did you come with as a long-term partner? Be specific.

13. What "baggage" came with your partner?

14. Do you have casual sex with other people? Does your partner?

15. Have you ever had an affair outside this relationship before?

16. Do you trust your partner to practice safe sex when making sexual contact outside the relationship? Why or why not?

17. Is your partner having an affair now? Are you certain? If yes, how do you feel about a third person in the relationship?

18. Do you or your partner try to justify your unfaithfulness? How?

19. Has this affair led to abuse or violence between you and your partner, or the third person in your triangle? If yes, describe the abuse or violence.

20. Do you think monogamy is necessary for the long-term relationship to last? Why?

21. Do you intend to stay in this long-term relationship, in spite of the affair?

22. Is this the first time betrayal has been present in your long-term relationship? If no, describe the previous incident(s). Why do you feel they began?

What were the consequences of straying for each of you in the love triangle?

▼ **You**

▼ **Your Long-Term Partner**

▼ **The New Lover (if you know that person)**

23. Do you and your partner know each other's feelings regarding unfaithfulness in your relationship? Do you understand each other's point of view? Do you respect those feelings? Explain your answer.

24. Has the affair changed your involvement in your hobbies or other things you enjoyed?

25. Has it affected your performance at work? Increased absenteeism? Fudging on expense accounts?

26. Would you and/or your partner be willing to seek counseling to help resolve your situation? If no, why not?

▼The New Lover in the Triangle

(Questions for men and women in affairs with lovers who are betraying their long-term partners.)

Your Lover

1. How and where did you meet your lover? Is he/she exclusively homosexual? Are you? _____

_____

2. Why did you choose this person? What was the attraction? Or did this person select you? _____

_____

3. Did you know your future lover was already committed to somebody else? _____

4. Is this your first affair with someone in a long-term relationship? If not, how many have there been? _____

5. How long has this affair been going on? _____

6. What limits and boundaries have you set regarding this affair? What limits and boundaries has your lover set? _____

_____

7. How do you contact your lover? Do you have his/her phone number and e-mail?

_____

8. How much time do you spend preparing for a rendezvous? What do you do to get ready? _____

_____

9. How much money have you spent on this affair? On what have you spent it (clothes, travel, hotels, gifts, meals, etc.)? _____

_____

10. Have these expenses been a financial hardship for you? Can you afford this?

_____

11. How much money has your lover spent on this affair? _____
On what has he/she spent it? _____

_____

_____

12. Does your lover allow the two of you to be seen together in public? _____

13. Has your lover introduced you to his/her friends — if yes, do they know you're his/her lover? _____

_____

_____

14. When do you see each other? Is it only during the week, or are you able to meet on weekends? How many times a week do you meet? _____

_____

15. Would you like to see more of each other? If yes, why don't you? _____

16. What is your favorite place to rendezvous? How does it make you feel to be there? _____

_____

17. Do the two of you practice safe sex? How can you be certain? _____

_____

18. Would you be attracted to each other if no sex were involved? _____

_____

_____

19. What stage would you say the affair is in:
  ▼ *New and Exciting*
  ▼ *In the Throes of Its Intensity* or
  ▼ *Burning Out and Nearing an End*?

Your Lover's Partner

20. Do you know your lover's long-term partner? _____

21. Does your lover's partner know about the affair? If yes, how does that complicate matters? Do you know how he/she found out? _____

_____

_____

22. If your lover's partner doesn't know, do you think he/she should be told? If yes, what's the purpose and who do you think should do it? _____

_____

_____

23. Do you have any reason to be fearful of your lover telling his/her long-term partner about the affair? If so, why? _____

_____

24. Do you expect your lover to break-up his/her long-term relationship? Why? _____

_____

25. How is this type of affair different from one with an uncommitted person? Why not select an unattached lover instead? _____

_____

Your Relationship

26. What qualities do you feel this person needs from you? _____

_____

27. What qualities do you need from your lover? _____

_____

28. Do you want this relationship to last indefinitely? Why or why not? _____

_____

29. Do you trust your lover? Why or why not? _____

30. Are you this person's only lover outside the partnership? If yes, how can you be certain? If no, do you know the others? _____

31. Do you feel you've changed during this relationship? If yes, how? Have there been changes in your lover? If yes, what? _____

_____

32. What do you feel is in this relationship for you now? Has that changed from the fantasies you envisioned in the beginning of the courtship? _____

_____

33. What are you risking by continuing this relationship? Can you afford the losses?

34. What do you feel is in this relationship for your lover — what's he/she getting out of it?

35. What is your lover risking in this relationship? Can he/she afford the possible losses?

36. Would you make a commitment to this person if the opportunity presented itself? Why?

37. How do you spend your free time when you're not with your lover?

38. How do you keep each other hooked in the affair? What keeps each of you coming back?

39. Are there patterns or cycles in this affair that tend to repeat themselves? If yes, what are they?

40. How would you describe your self-esteem today? Has it changed in the last year?

41. What lies do you feel your lover tells his/her partner?

42. What lies do you feel your lover tells you?

43. What lies have you told your lover?

▼For Every Part of the Triangle

How has this affair affected these vital aspects of your life?

Emotions

Physical Health

Family Life

Communication

Finances

Job Performance

General Quality of Life

▼ ▼ ▼ *creative* writing 101

No More Cover-Ups!

No More Cover-Ups!

**the one doing the
cheating (betrayer)**

the new lover

the one
being
betrayed

This section is for the Gay or Lesbian being betrayed.

*(If you're **The One Doing the Cheating** or if you're **The New Lover**, skip ahead to one of the next two sections.)*

Using the space provided:

1. Write a letter to the two other sides of your triangle: your partner and his or her new lover. The purpose of this exercise is to finally let these people know what you're going through as a direct result of the betrayal. Don't hold back. Express your anger and your hurt. Share whatever is on your mind. Remember, *you're not going to deliver these letters*, so be completely upfront.

In all cases, let the other players know what you are feeling, **what you consider to be unfair about your situation, how you want things to work out in the long run, and anything else that's important.**

Pretend you are face-to-face.

To your partner:

To your partner's lover:

2. It's time to write a letter to yourself — just for you.

Take a good look at your situation as you write a letter full of advice. Express your pain, concerns, anger and sense of loss regarding your lover's betrayal. How do you feel after letting them have a piece of your mind?

(Remember to list your options and what is best for you in the long run.) _____

_____

_____

_____

_____

_____

_____

_____

_____

_____

_____

_____

_____

_____

_____

_____

_____

_____

3. The Pressure is Mounting! Devise a plan *to overcome the odds.*

a) List three things you *could* do, realistically, to help yourself at this time.

1. _____

2. _____

3. _____

b) Working from your list, what could go wrong if you tried these plans?

1. _____

2. _____

3. _____

c) Working from your list, what would you gain if you carried out these ideas?

1. _____

2. _____

3. _____

d) Working from your list, what prevents you from trying them immediately?

1. _____

2. _____

3. _____

e) What can you do *right now* to help yourself the most? _____

_____

_____

_____

_____

4. Write some classified ads, for the "Personals" section of the newspaper, which you *don't* intend to place. Keep them short and to the point.

a) Write an ad offering to turn over your role as the betrayed person in this triangle to someone else. **Invite a willing taker to step into your shoes.** Include any important warnings regarding the consequences to expect.

b) Compose an ad that you want the other two players (your cheating partner and his/her lover) in your love triangle to find. Give revealing details, without using names. Inform the other players of what you want and what you expect them to do to improve your situation *now. They should have no problem identifying you as the person who placed the ad.*

5. Complete the following assessments:

a) Describe yourself prior to the intrusion of this person (your partner's new lover) into your relationship. What were you like? How did you feel then and what was the relationship between you and your partner? _____

_____

_____

_____

b) Write a description of yourself now, in the throes of this nightmare. Include your feelings, concerns and what you want changed immediately. Share where you think your situation is headed and how you can best protect yourself because of it.

_____

_____

_____

c) Okay, your partner's affair has finally ended. Describe your feelings now, after the ordeal. List the lessons you have learned and share the mistakes you do not care to repeat. What are your plans now? _____

_____

_____

_____

d) It's been three months since the affair has ended. Are you and your partner together? If so, how are the two of you doing? Is the relationship stronger or weaker? What are you doing to prevent this from happening again? _____

_____

_____

_____

No More Cover-Ups!

**the one being
betrayed**

the new lover

the one
doing the
cheating
(the betrayer)

This section is for The One Doing The Cheating. (The Betrayer)

(If you're *The New Lover,* skip ahead to the next section.)

Using the space provided:

1. Write two letters — one to your long-term partner and one to your lover. The purpose is to finally let these people know your thoughts and real intentions. Share why you decided to step out and stray. Don't hold back. Express your feelings. Remember, *you are not going to deliver these letters*. There's no need to be concerned about how you look or how your letter affects the others in your love triangle.

Let them know exactly what they can expect from you and why you chose this path.

Say the things you don't plan to say face-to-face.

It is time:

To your long-term partner:

To your new lover:

2. Write a letter to yourself. What are the consequences of your unfaithfulness, and where are you now as it relates to both your long-term partner and your new lover? Include your regrets and lessons learned, if any.

3. Prepare the following classified ads, which you *don't* intend to place.
   Keep them short and to the point.

As the betrayer, write an ad offering to turn over your role in this triangle to someone else. Invite a willing taker to step into your shoes from the beginning of the affair, in the throes of it, or at whichever point you choose. Sell the benefits, but also include important warnings and consequences they can expect.

Compose an ad that describes both your long-term partner and your new lover. Don't be afraid to share what's on your mind. If this were in a gay/lesbian newsletter or magazine, the reader should be able to identify who the ad is about, without revealing names.

4. Complete the following assessments:

   a) Describe yourself prior to bringing a new lover into your relationship.
Why did you choose this person? What were the circumstances that led up to your unfaithfulness?

_____

_____

_____

_____

   b) Briefly describe yourself now, in the throes of this new relationship.
Share your feelings regarding your long-term partner and your new lover. What are your intentions now regarding each of them? What do you want to change? Assess where you see this situation going.

_____

_____

_____

_____

   c) Okay, your affair has finally ended. What are your plans?
List them and your strategies for making them become your reality. What are the mistakes and consequences you do not intend to repeat?

_____

_____

_____

_____

   d) It's been three months since the affair has ended.
How are you and your partner doing now? Is the relationship stronger or weaker? Presuming you are still with one another, have each of you healed and recovered? What are you and your partner doing to prevent this from happening again?

_____

_____

_____

_____

notes

No More Cover-Ups!

**the one doing the
cheating (the betrayer)**

**the one being
betrayed**

the
new
lover

This section is for The New Lover

Using the space provided:

1. The purpose is to finally let these people know what you are going through as you share *your* perspective. Write two letters — one to your lover and one to your lover's long-term partner. Share why you became involved and have stayed in this relationship. Let each of them know what you expect as the new lover. Include why you chose to be in this affair with someone already "taken." State *any* concerns you have.

Don't hold back. Express your frustrations, anger and sadness about your predicament. **Remember, you're not going to deliver these letters**.

Get it all out!

To your lover:

To your lover's long-term partner:

2. Write a letter to yourself. It's time to re-evaluate your current situation.

What will you feel like if your lover returns to his or her long-term partner? This letter should include **your course of action.**

3. Write the following classified ads that you *will not* place.
   Keep them direct and to the point.

Write an ad offering to turn over your role as the new lover in this triangle to someone else. Invite a willing taker to step into your shoes. Sell possible benefits, but also include important warnings and consequences they can expect to inherit.

Create an ad you want your lover and his or her long-term partner to find. Give revealing details, without using names. Let them know what you want them to do to improve the situation immediately.

4. Complete the following assessments:

a) Describe yourself *prior to this relationship*. What circumstances led up to this affair? Is this your first or one of several? _____

_____

_____

_____

b) Assess yourself now, *in the throes of this new relationship*. Describe how you feel when your lover returns home to his/her long-term partner. Are you seeing other people? Romantically? Have your feelings and motives changed from when you first became involved? What are the advantages and disadvantages of being in your position? _____

_____

_____

_____

c) Okay, your affair has ended. Where are you headed? Are you intending to become involved in another affair or will you break the cycle of betrayal as you begin to assess the damage? _____

_____

_____

_____

d) It's been three months since the affair has ended. Are you still together? What are you doing to **prevent** this situation from happening again? _____

_____

_____

_____

_____

notes

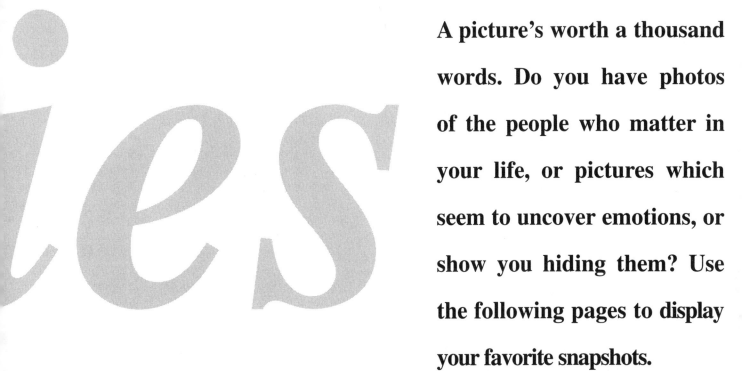

▼ ▼ ▼

photo
gallery

memories

A picture's worth a thousand words. Do you have photos of the people who matter in your life, or pictures which seem to uncover emotions, or show you hiding them? Use the following pages to display your favorite snapshots.

daily entries...

Your Affair's Progression

Fill in the month, week and day of your entry (i.e., Month 1, Week 1, Day 1). Then just write in the blanks each day.

daily entry *glossary*

Refer to the following terms as you fill-in your Daily Entry categories.

Abuse

Is anyone in the triangle being abused physically? (Emotional abuse occurs just by the circumstances of betrayal.) Do arguments escalate to shoving matches or worse? Whether you are being abused, doing the abusing, or observing the abuse, it hurts and can become a habit. Physical abuse cannot be shrugged off, as patterns can develop quickly. Use this section to keep track of it.
A reminder: **GET HELP NOW.**

Accountability

You're accountable to anyone who is deceived by you, or who is compromised by your involvement in this triangle: *yourself, your partner, your lover(s), your coworkers, your friends.*

Broken Promises

Did someone cancel plans at the last minute? Were you told the affair would end by now, but it has not? Are you breaking promises and not meeting deadlines? This is where you write down any and all of the day's broken promises.

Contact and Time

Did you see your lover today? If no, why not? Was there any communication? How long has it been since you last talked, saw each other, made love?

How much time did you devote to this relationship today? How did you spend it? Getting yourself ready for a rendezvous…face-to-face contact…shopping for things you hope will impress your lover...wishing you were together...worrying about the situation…talking on the phone…waiting for it to ring…discussing the relationship with a friend…exchanging e-mail...attending therapy....

Fears, Frustrations and Disappointments

What were you most afraid of today? What are the things this affair could lead to that you would most like to avoid? Share your frustrations and disappointments.

Forgiveness

"To err is human. To forgive is divine."
Use this space to forgive those who have hurt you and list those whom you have hurt. Recovery permits forgiveness, fostering growth and closure.

Hopes and Fantasies

If you could change anything about your situation, what would it be today? Are your hopes and fantasies the same? Write them down every day because they have a way of changing, as well as keeping you trapped.

Lies

Use this category to write down the lies *you* told today, the lies your lover told you and the lies that others are telling for you concerning your affair. Include the lies you tell yourself.

Patterns

Use this space to help identify specific patterns in your relationship that keep repeating themselves. How do you feel about them recurring? What do you think they say about the affair?

Realities

What did you discover or were you reminded of today that stands between you and your hopes and fantasies?
Realities can be things like,
"He will never stop *fooling around…*"
"She loves her more each day…"
"He only wants me for the sex…"
"She'll tell me anything to keep me hooked…"
"This lover is really someone else's life-long partner..."

Regrets and Amends

What happened today that you wish hadn't? What are the things you wish you had done differently? These are the *should-ofs*, the *what-ifs*. Keep track of them.

Affairs leave a wake of pain and sorrow. Use this space to describe what you've done or intend to do to make amends and to whom. Include those people you feel owe amends to you.

Risks

Typical risks include having your affair exposed, the wrong people finding out, losing your self-respect, spending hard-earned money that you could put to other uses, losing your job for missing work or performing poorly, as well as damage to your good name and reputation. Are you wasting promising years of your life and missing out on the things you would be doing if you weren't in this situation? Are you at risk of losing your partner and your lover?

Silver Linings

Every cloud has one.... Your situation is probably far from ideal. Regardless of how it's progressing, list what you're grateful for today.

Thoughts for the Day

Write straight from your heart. Say what is on your mind.

Ultimatums, Limits and Boundaries

Eventually most affairs accumulate a number of ultimatums — "End it or I'm calling your lover…" "No more free rides…" "If you ever see him/her again, I'm leaving…" Ultimatums take on many forms and tend to change over time. This is where you write down the terms you gave today and those that were given to you. Did you follow through on what you said you would do?

Affairs create certain limits and boundaries for both of you. They tend to change as the affair evolves. Basically, they're the rules that you agree on — "Don't tell a soul…" "Never call the house…" "I want to know everything…" This is where you write down any changes in the *limits and boundaries,* and record any violations.

daily entries...

Fill in the month, week and day of your entry
(i.e., Month 1, Week 1, Day 1).
Then just write in the blanks, one day at a time.

Month _____

Week _____

Day _____

Contact and Time _____

_____

_____

Fears, Frustrations & Disappointments _____

_____

_____

Risks _____

_____

_____

Lies _____

_____

_____

Broken Promises _____

_____

_____

Abuse _____

_____

_____

Ultimatums, Limits & Boundaries _____

_____

_____

Patterns

Hopes & Fantasies

Realities

Accountability

Regrets & Amends

Forgiveness

Silver Linings

Thoughts for the Day

Month

Week

Day

Contact and Time

Fears, Frustrations & Disappointments

Risks

Lies

Broken Promises

Abuse

Ultimatums, Limits & Boundaries

Patterns _____

_____

_____

Hopes & Fantasies _____

_____

_____

Realities _____

_____

_____

Accountability _____

_____

_____

Regrets & Amends _____

_____

_____

Forgiveness _____

_____

_____

Silver Linings _____

_____

_____

Thoughts for the Day _____

_____

_____

Month _____

Week _____

Day _____

Contact and Time _____

_____

_____

Fears, Frustrations & Disappointments _____

_____

_____

Risks _____

_____

_____

Lies _____

_____

_____

Broken Promises _____

_____

_____

Abuse _____

_____

_____

Ultimatums, Limits & Boundaries _____

_____

_____

Patterns

Hopes & Fantasies

Realities

Accountability

Regrets & Amends

Forgiveness

Silver Linings

Thoughts for the Day

Month _____

Week _____

Day _____

Contact and Time _____

_____

_____

Fears, Frustrations & Disappointments _____

_____

_____

Risks _____

_____

_____

Lies _____

_____

_____

Broken Promises _____

_____

_____

Abuse _____

_____

_____

Ultimatums, Limits & Boundaries _____

_____

_____

Patterns

Hopes & Fantasies

Realities

Accountability

Regrets & Amends

Forgiveness

Silver Linings

Thoughts for the Day

Month

Week

Day

Contact and Time

Fears, Frustrations & Disappointments

Risks

Lies

Broken Promises

Abuse

Ultimatums, Limits & Boundaries

Patterns

Hopes & Fantasies

Realities

Accountability

Regrets & Amends

Forgiveness

Silver Linings

Thoughts for the Day

Month _____

Week _____

Day _____

Contact and Time _____

_____

_____

Fears, Frustrations & Disappointments _____

_____

_____

Risks _____

_____

_____

Lies _____

_____

_____

Broken Promises _____

_____

_____

Abuse _____

_____

_____

Ultimatums, Limits & Boundaries _____

_____

_____

Patterns

Hopes & Fantasies

Realities

Accountability

Regrets & Amends

Forgiveness

Silver Linings

Thoughts for the Day

Month _____

Week _____

Day _____

Contact and Time _____

_____

_____

Fears, Frustrations & Disappointments _____

_____

_____

Risks _____

_____

_____

Lies _____

_____

_____

Broken Promises _____

_____

_____

Abuse _____

_____

_____

Ultimatums, Limits & Boundaries _____

_____

_____

Patterns

Hopes & Fantasies

Realities

Accountability

Regrets & Amends

Forgiveness

Silver Linings

Thoughts for the Day

Month _____

Week _____

Day _____

Contact and Time _____

_____

_____

Fears, Frustrations & Disappointments _____

_____

_____

Risks _____

_____

_____

Lies _____

_____

_____

Broken Promises _____

_____

_____

Abuse _____

_____

_____

Ultimatums, Limits & Boundaries _____

_____

_____

Patterns

Hopes & Fantasies

Realities

Accountability

Regrets & Amends

Forgiveness

Silver Linings

Thoughts for the Day

Month

Week

Day

Contact and Time

Fears, Frustrations & Disappointments

Risks

Lies

Broken Promises

Abuse

Ultimatums, Limits & Boundaries

Patterns

Hopes & Fantasies

Realities

Accountability

Regrets & Amends

Forgiveness

Silver Linings

Thoughts for the Day

Month

Week

Day

Contact and Time

Fears, Frustrations & Disappointments

Risks

Lies

Broken Promises

Abuse

Ultimatums, Limits & Boundaries

Patterns

Hopes & Fantasies

Realities

Accountability

Regrets & Amends

Forgiveness

Silver Linings

Thoughts for the Day

Month _____

Week _____

Day _____

Contact and Time _____

_____

_____

Fears, Frustrations & Disappointments _____

_____

_____

Risks _____

_____

_____

Lies _____

_____

_____

Broken Promises _____

_____

_____

Abuse _____

_____

_____

Ultimatums, Limits & Boundaries _____

_____

_____

Patterns

Hopes & Fantasies

Realities

Accountability

Regrets & Amends

Forgiveness

Silver Linings

Thoughts for the Day

Month _____

Week _____

Day _____

Contact and Time _____

_____

_____

Fears, Frustrations & Disappointments _____

_____

_____

Risks _____

_____

_____

Lies _____

_____

_____

Broken Promises _____

_____

_____

Abuse _____

_____

_____

Ultimatums, Limits & Boundaries _____

_____

_____

Patterns

Hopes & Fantasies

Realities

Accountability

Regrets & Amends

Forgiveness

Silver Linings

Thoughts for the Day

Month

Week

Day

Contact and Time

Fears, Frustrations & Disappointments

Risks

Lies

Broken Promises

Abuse

Ultimatums, Limits & Boundaries

Patterns

Hopes & Fantasies

Realities

Accountability

Regrets & Amends

Forgiveness

Silver Linings

Thoughts for the Day

Month

Week

Day

Contact and Time

Fears, Frustrations & Disappointments

Risks

Lies

Broken Promises

Abuse

Ultimatums, Limits & Boundaries

Patterns

Hopes & Fantasies

Realities

Accountability

Regrets & Amends

Forgiveness

Silver Linings

Thoughts for the Day

Month ....
Week ....
Day ....

Contact and Time ....

....

....

Fears, Frustrations & Disappointments ....

....

....

Risks ....

....

....

Lies ....

....

....

Broken Promises ....

....

....

Abuse ....

....

....

Ultimatums, Limits & Boundaries ....

....

....

Patterns

Hopes & Fantasies

Realities

Accountability

Regrets & Amends

Forgiveness

Silver Linings

Thoughts for the Day

Month _____

Week _____

Day _____

Contact and Time _____

_____

_____

Fears, Frustrations & Disappointments _____

_____

_____

Risks _____

_____

_____

Lies _____

_____

_____

Broken Promises _____

_____

_____

Abuse _____

_____

_____

Ultimatums, Limits & Boundaries _____

_____

_____

Patterns

Hopes & Fantasies

Realities

Accountability

Regrets & Amends

Forgiveness

Silver Linings

Thoughts for the Day

Month

Week

Day

Contact and Time

Fears, Frustrations & Disappointments

Risks

Lies

Broken Promises

Abuse

Ultimatums, Limits & Boundaries

Patterns

Hopes & Fantasies

Realities

Accountability

Regrets & Amends

Forgiveness

Silver Linings

Thoughts for the Day

Month ....

Week ....

Day ....

Contact and Time ....

....

....

Fears, Frustrations & Disappointments ....

....

....

Risks ....

....

....

Lies ....

....

....

Broken Promises ....

....

....

Abuse ....

....

....

Ultimatums, Limits & Boundaries ....

....

....

Patterns

Hopes & Fantasies

Realities

Accountability

Regrets & Amends

Forgiveness

Silver Linings

Thoughts for the Day

Month

Week

Day

Contact and Time

Fears, Frustrations & Disappointments

Risks

Lies

Broken Promises

Abuse

Ultimatums, Limits & Boundaries

Patterns

Hopes & Fantasies

Realities

Accountability

Regrets & Amends

Forgiveness

Silver Linings

Thoughts for the Day

Month

Week

Day

Contact and Time

Fears, Frustrations & Disappointments

Risks

Lies

Broken Promises

Abuse

Ultimatums, Limits & Boundaries

Patterns

Hopes & Fantasies

Realities

Accountability

Regrets & Amends

Forgiveness

Silver Linings

Thoughts for the Day

Month

Week

Day

Contact and Time

Fears, Frustrations & Disappointments

Risks

Lies

Broken Promises

Abuse

Ultimatums, Limits & Boundaries

Patterns

Hopes & Fantasies

Realities

Accountability

Regrets & Amends

Forgiveness

Silver Linings

Thoughts for the Day

Month

Week

Day

Contact and Time

Fears, Frustrations & Disappointments

Risks

Lies

Broken Promises

Abuse

Ultimatums, Limits & Boundaries

Patterns

Hopes & Fantasies

Realities

Accountability

Regrets & Amends

Forgiveness

Silver Linings

Thoughts for the Day

Month _____

Week _____

Day _____

Contact and Time _____

_____

_____

Fears, Frustrations & Disappointments _____

_____

_____

Risks _____

_____

_____

Lies _____

_____

_____

Broken Promises _____

_____

_____

Abuse _____

_____

_____

Ultimatums, Limits & Boundaries _____

_____

_____

Patterns

Hopes & Fantasies

Realities

Accountability

Regrets & Amends

Forgiveness

Silver Linings

Thoughts for the Day

Month _____

Week _____

Day _____

Contact and Time _____

_____

_____

Fears, Frustrations & Disappointments _____

_____

_____

Risks _____

_____

_____

Lies _____

_____

_____

Broken Promises _____

_____

_____

Abuse _____

_____

_____

Ultimatums, Limits & Boundaries _____

_____

_____

Patterns

Hopes & Fantasies

Realities

Accountability

Regrets & Amends

Forgiveness

Silver Linings

Thoughts for the Day

Month _____

Week _____

Day _____

Contact and Time _____

_____

_____

Fears, Frustrations & Disappointments _____

_____

_____

Risks _____

_____

_____

Lies _____

_____

_____

Broken Promises _____

_____

_____

Abuse _____

_____

_____

Ultimatums, Limits & Boundaries _____

_____

_____

Patterns

Hopes & Fantasies

Realities

Accountability

Regrets & Amends

Forgiveness

Silver Linings

Thoughts for the Day

Month _____

Week _____

Day _____

Contact and Time _____

_____

_____

Fears, Frustrations & Disappointments _____

_____

_____

Risks _____

_____

_____

Lies _____

_____

_____

Broken Promises _____

_____

_____

Abuse _____

_____

_____

Ultimatums, Limits & Boundaries _____

_____

Patterns

Hopes & Fantasies

Realities

Accountability

Regrets & Amends

Forgiveness

Silver Linings

Thoughts for the Day

Month _____

Week _____

Day _____

Contact and Time _____

_____

_____

Fears, Frustrations & Disappointments _____

_____

_____

Risks _____

_____

_____

Lies _____

_____

_____

Broken Promises _____

_____

_____

Abuse _____

_____

_____

Ultimatums, Limits & Boundaries _____

_____

Patterns

Hopes & Fantasies

Realities

Accountability

Regrets & Amends

Forgiveness

Silver Linings

Thoughts for the Day

the gay and lesbian journal

Month _____

Week _____

Day _____

Contact and Time _____

Fears, Frustrations & Disappointments _____

Risks _____

Lies _____

Broken Promises _____

Abuse _____

Ultimatums, Limits & Boundaries _____

Patterns

Hopes & Fantasies

Realities

Accountability

Regrets & Amends

Forgiveness

Silver Linings

Thoughts for the Day

Month _____

Week _____

Day _____

Contact and Time _____

_____

_____

Fears, Frustrations & Disappointments _____

_____

_____

Risks _____

_____

_____

Lies _____

_____

_____

Broken Promises _____

_____

_____

Abuse _____

_____

_____

Ultimatums, Limits & Boundaries _____

_____

_____

Patterns

Hopes & Fantasies

Realities

Accountability

Regrets & Amends

Forgiveness

Silver Linings

Thoughts for the Day

Month _____

Week _____

Day _____

Contact and Time _____

_____

_____

Fears, Frustrations & Disappointments _____

_____

_____

Risks _____

_____

_____

Lies _____

_____

_____

Broken Promises _____

_____

_____

Abuse _____

_____

_____

Ultimatums, Limits & Boundaries _____

_____

_____

Patterns

Hopes & Fantasies

Realities

Accountability

Regrets & Amends

Forgiveness

Silver Linings

Thoughts for the Day

Month _____

Week _____

Day _____

Contact and Time _____

_____

_____

Fears, Frustrations & Disappointments _____

_____

_____

Risks _____

_____

_____

Lies _____

_____

_____

Broken Promises _____

_____

_____

Abuse _____

_____

_____

Ultimatums, Limits & Boundaries _____

_____

_____

Patterns

Hopes & Fantasies

Realities

Accountability

Regrets & Amends

Forgiveness

Silver Linings

Thoughts for the Day

How to contact
FACE REALITY™

Face Reality offers a selection of products and services intended to help you place your past, present or future — in — way. These are available in a variety of means. Look over the current list and contact Face Reality in any of the following ways for more information or to place an order. This journal and ass—

How to *contact* FACE REALITY

A selection of products and services intended to help individuals face the facts about betrayal are available. Look over the current list and contact Face Reality in any of the following ways for more information or to place an order.

This journal and the associated materials are in no way substitutes for professional counseling and/or therapy. They act as their companions. I am a strong advocate of professional help and a testimony to its positive effectiveness.

Face Reality welcomes your feedback. Please feel free to share your experience and your story of recovery by faxing or writing to us.

Face Reality™ Resources

▼ *Infidelity and You*

This book presents proven solutions for coping with unfaithfulness for individuals affected in a variety of ways — the spouse or partner, a child or other family member, the "other man" or the "other woman," or the gay or lesbian lover. You'll learn what motivates betrayal and how to prevent it. A significant portion of the book also addresses suggestions on how to identify a troubled marriage or relationship and what can be done to restore it.

▼ Self-Reflecting Journals

Keeping a journal tailored to your particular situation can be important in your overall healing and recovery.

Order the journal best suited to your situation.

A *WOMAN'S* GUIDE TO (AND FROM) INFIDELITY
    The Journal for Wives Whose Husbands Cheat on Them and for
    Wives Who Cheat on Their Husbands (or would like to)
A *MAN'S* GUIDE TO (AND FROM) INFIDELITY
    The Journal for Husbands Who Cheat on their Wives (or would like to)
    and for Husbands Whose Wives Cheat on Them
THE *OTHER WOMAN'S* GUIDE TO (AND FROM) INFIDELITY
    The Journal for Women in Affairs with Married Men
THE *OTHER MAN'S* GUIDE TO (AND FROM) INFIDELITY
    The Journal for Men in Affairs with Married Women
THE *TEEN'S* COPING GUIDE TO A PARENT'S INFIDELITY
    The Journal for Teens Caught Up in Their Parent's Extramarital Affairs
THE *GAY AND LESBIAN* GUIDE TO (AND FROM) BETRAYAL
    The Journal for Gays & Lesbians Suffering the Pains of a Love Triangle

▼ Audio Tapes

These tapes speak directly to your circumstances. They can be listened to in the privacy of your home, your car or while you're exercising. They cover some of the most poignant issues that you might be facing. Narrated by Elissa Gough.

▼ Contact Face Reality On the Internet:

Contact us by email: **info@facereality.com**

▼ Visit Face Reality™ on the World Wide Web

If you are among the growing millions with access to the Internet, visit us on the World Wide Web. Our address is:

http://www.facereality.com

You'll find complete information on all the services and products we offer. There are chat rooms where you can hold confidential discussions with others from around the country and the world, in situations similar to yours.

▼ Seminars/Workshops/Retreats/Support Groups

Seminars, workshops and retreats led by Elissa Gough are available to you. Whether you're the husband, wife, other man or woman, gay partner or the child of a cheating parent, a program can be designed to your specific needs.

▼ Professional Care-Givers (Referrals and Workshops)

If you're looking for new concepts to help your clients, I would like to include you in my network of care-giver referrals. Only currently licensed, practicing care-givers need respond.

▼ Corporate Consulting Services

Infidelity continues to soar in the workplace. Are you an employer whose work environment has been or is currently being affected by infidelity? We can help you take steps to minimize this problem.

▼ By Mail:

Face Reality, Inc.
P.O. Box 8593
Cincinnati, Ohio 45208-0593

▼ By Phone or Fax:

To order Face Reality products: 1-800-5AFFAIR

For information on Face Reality seminars and consulting services, call or fax our business office:

Monday through Friday
9 a.m. to 5 p.m. EST
1-513-871-4999

notes

notes

notes

ORDER FORM

Telephone orders Call Toll Free:

1-800 -5AFFAIR
Fax orders: (513) 871-4999
Postal orders: Face Reality, Inc., P.O. Box 8593
Cincinnati, OH 45208-0593

FACE REALITY ™

Order online at:
http://www.facereality.com

Name_____

Address_____

City_____State____Zip_____

Telephone (_ _ _) _ _ _ — _ _ _ _

PAYMENT ☐ Check or Money Order Enclosed

Charge my   ☐ Visa   ☐ MC   ☐ Discover

| | | | | | | | | | | | | | | | | | | | | | | |
Card Number   Exp. Date

_____
Signature

ORDER INFORMATION

Item	Title	Qty.	Price ea.	Total
☐	Infidelity & You		$14.95	
☐	Woman's Journal		$19.95	
☐	Other Woman's Journal		$19.95	
☐	Man's Journal		$19.95	
☐	Other Man's Journal		$19.95	
☐	Gay & Lesbian Journal		$19.95	
☐	The Teen's Journal		$19.95	
☐	Face Reality on Tape		$ 9.95	

Quantity discounts are available on bulk purchases of these materials for both educational purposes and fund raising.

Merchandise Total_____
Shipping Charges $ 4.95
Subtotal_____
6% Sales Tax on Subtotal
(OH only)_____
Order Total_____

These materials are in no way a substitute for professional counseling and/or therapy. They act as their companion. I am a strong advocate of professional help and a testimony to its positive effectiveness.

Elissa Gough